NORTH AMERICAN ANIMALS

Jackrabbits

by Christina Leaf

BLASTOFF!
3
READERS

Note to Librarians, Teachers, and Parents:

Blastoff! Readers are carefully developed by literacy experts and combine standards-based content with developmentally appropriate text.

Level 1 provides the most support through repetition of high-frequency words, light text, predictable sentence patterns, and strong visual support.

Level 2 offers early readers a bit more challenge through varied simple sentences, increased text load, and less repetition of high-frequency words.

Level 3 advances early-fluent readers toward fluency through increased text and concept load, less reliance on visuals, longer sentences, and more literary language.

Level 4 builds reading stamina by providing more text per page, increased use of punctuation, greater variation in sentence patterns, and increasingly challenging vocabulary.

Level 5 encourages children to move from "learning to read" to "reading to learn" by providing even more text, varied writing styles, and less familiar topics.

Whichever book is right for your reader, Blastoff! Readers are the perfect books to build confidence and encourage a love of reading that will last a lifetime!

This edition first published in 2015 by Bellwether Media, Inc.

No part of this publication may be reproduced in whole or in part without written permission of the publisher. For information regarding permission, write to Bellwether Media, Inc., Attention: Permissions Department, 5357 Penn Avenue South, Minneapolis, MN 55419.

Library of Congress Cataloging-in-Publication Data

Leaf, Christina.
Jackrabbits / by Christina Leaf.
    pages cm. – (Blastoff! Readers. North American Animals)
Includes bibliographical references and index.
Summary: "Simple text and full-color photography introduce beginning readers to jackrabbits. Developed by literacy experts for students in kindergarten through third grade"– Provided by publisher.
Audience: Ages 5-8
Audience: K to Grade 3.
ISBN 978-1-62617-191-6 (hardcover : alk. paper)
1. Jackrabbits–Juvenile literature. I. Title.
QL737.L32L44 2015
599.32'8–dc23

2014040277

Table of Contents

What Are Jackrabbits?

Jackrabbits are a type of **hare**. These **mammals** are found across the western and central United States.

In the Wild

N
W • E
S

Extinct

Extinct in the Wild

Critically Endangered

Endangered

Vulnerable

Near Threatened

Least Concern

jackrabbit range =

conservation status: least concern

They also live in northern Mexico and southwestern Canada.

Jackrabbits like open **habitats**. Prairies and fields are homes for many.

In southern areas, jackrabbits are found in **desert scrublands**. In the far north, they may live in **tundra**.

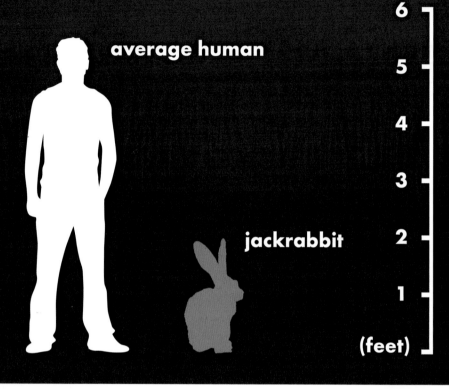

Size of a Jackrabbit

average human

jackrabbit

6

5

4

3

2

1

(feet)

Jackrabbits look a lot like rabbits. However, they are larger in size. They are about 2 feet (0.6 meters) long.

Bigger body parts also set jackrabbits apart. They have longer ears, back legs, and back feet than rabbits.

Identify a Jackrabbit

large ears

long back legs and feet

Most jackrabbits have brownish gray coats. However, their tails are not all the same color. Some have white tails. Others have tails with a dark stripe.

White-tailed jackrabbits can change color with the seasons. They may turn white in winter to blend in with snow.

Finding Food

Jackrabbits spend their days eating. These animals are **herbivores**.

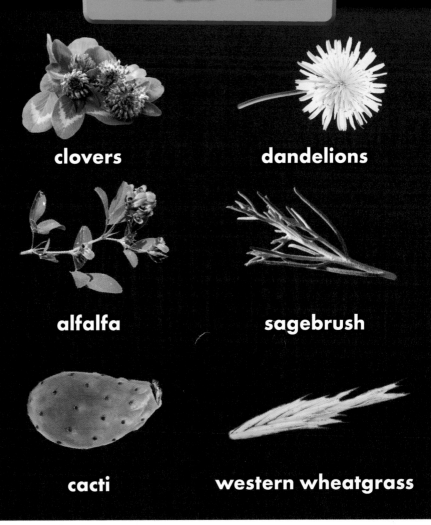

clovers

dandelions

alfalfa

sagebrush

cacti

western wheatgrass

They nibble on grasses, buds, and other plants. Sometimes they chew on bark and twigs.

Many animals hunt jackrabbits. The hares must watch and listen for **raptors**, wildcats, and other **predators**.

red foxes

mountain lions

coyotes

bobcats

red-tailed hawks

golden eagles

Their springy legs allow them to escape from danger with long bounds.

Jackrabbits also move quickly at speeds up to 40 miles per hour (64 kilometers per hour). They **zigzag** so they are harder to catch.

Female jackrabbits have several litters in a year. They give birth to **leverets** in grassy holes or on the ground. Unlike rabbits, they do not build nests.

Baby Facts

Name for babies:	leverets
Size of litter:	1 to 6 leverets
Length of pregnancy:	30 to 45 days
Time spent with mom:	3 to 4 weeks

Leverets are born with open eyes and all their fur.

They do not need much care from mom. The babies can hop around soon after birth!

Glossary

desert scrublands—dry lands with short bushes and trees

habitats—lands with certain types of plants, animals, and weather

hare—a fast animal that looks like a rabbit but with larger ears and back legs

herbivores—animals that only eat plants

leverets—baby jackrabbits

mammals—warm-blooded animals that have backbones and feed their young milk

predators—animals that hunt other animals for food

raptors—large birds that hunt other animals; raptors have excellent eyesight and powerful talons.

tundra—dry land where the ground is frozen year-round

zigzag—to move in a path that has short, sharp turns

To Learn More

AT THE LIBRARY
Irbinskas, Heather. *How Jackrabbit Got His Very Long Ears.* Flagstaff, Ariz.: Northland Pub., 1994.

Leach, Michael. *Hare.* New York, N.Y.: PowerKids Press, 2009.

Robbins, Lynette. *Rabbits and Hares.* New York, N.Y.: PowerKids Press, 2012.

ON THE WEB
Learning more about jackrabbits is as easy as 1, 2, 3.

1. Go to www.factsurfer.com.

2. Enter "jackrabbits" into the search box.

3. Click the "Surf" button and you will see a list of related web sites.

With factsurfer.com, finding more information is just a click away.

Index

The images in this book are reproduced through the courtesy of: Ingrid Curry, front cover; Twildlife, pp. 4-5; NaturePL/ SuperStock, p. 6; Henry Ausloos/ Photononstop/ Glow Images, pp. 6-7; Tom & Pat Leeson/ KimballStock, pp. 8-9; Jouko van der Kruijssen/ Corbis, p. 10 (top left); Steven Love, p. 10 (bottom left); Rick & Nora Bowers/ Alamy, pp. 10 (right), 16; Donald M. Jones/ Corbis, p. 11; Gerlach Nature Photography/ Age Fotostock, pp. 12-13; Scisetti Alfio, p. 13 (top left, bottom left); Quang Ho, p. 13 (top right); Kazakov Maksim, p. 13 (center left); Kerry V. McQuaid, p. 13 (center right); Sheri Hagwood/ USDA, p. 13 (bottom right); Dan Sullivan/ Alamy, pp. 14-15; Eric Isselee, p. 15 (top left); Ultrashock, p. 15 (top right); Cynthia Kidwell, p. 15 (center left); Svetlana Foote, p. 15 (center right); Le Do, p. 15 (bottom left); Juan Martinez, p. 15 (bottom right); Jaymi Heimbuch/ Alamy, p. 17; Damon Clarke, pp. 18, 20; Design Pics/ SuperStock, p. 19; Denise Coyle, p. 21.